Original title:
Candles, Carols, and Christmas Eve

Copyright © 2024 Creative Arts Management OÜ
All rights reserved.

Author: Atticus Thornton
ISBN HARDBACK: 978-9916-90-886-0
ISBN PAPERBACK: 978-9916-90-887-7

Snowflakes on Serenades

Flakes of laughter fall with cheer,
Hats askew, we dance near.

Wobbly moves in twinkling glow,
Cousins spin in a blustery show.

Socks are mismatched, we don't care,
Jokes and giggles fill the air.

Snow men topple, oh what a sight,
As we tumble in pure delight.

Euphoria at Dusk

Jingle bells are out of tune,
Uncle Fred is howling at the moon.

Chaos reigns as cookies burn,
Flour fights take a sudden turn.

Pine cone crafts that make no sense,
A reindeer dressed in wide defense.

Drinks in cups with much too foam,
Everyone's singing, 'Take me home!'

Festival of Lights

Strangled lights on the big tree,
Grandpa blushes, 'That's not me!'

Shiny tinsel hangs askew,
Kids are plotting mischief too.

Nuts are cracking in the air,
A cat's leaping without a care.

Holiday songs from the wrong tune,
Giggles echo, 'We'll change it soon!'

Wishes on the Breeze

Plates piled high, a feast awaits,
A game of charades, oh the fate!

Auntie's wig falls, laughter bursts,
Hot cocoa challenges quench our thirst.

Wishing stars drift on our breath,
Silly dances, the spirit of heft.

Merriment swirls like the frost,
In these moments, we're never lost.

Whimsy in the Night

In the glow of twinkling lights,
The cat's climbing higher, oh what sights!
A leg of ham is now a toy,
As mice sing loud in purest joy.

The cookies left are nibbled through,
A bite for Santa, one for you.
The reindeer prance with silly glee,
Dancing on roofs like it's a spree.

Hearts Alight with Joy

The stockings hang with quirky flair,
One stuffed with socks and some pet hair.
The laughter echoes far and wide,
As uncle Fred spills punch with pride.

The tree's adorned with colors bright,
A squirrel tries to take a bite.
We sing off-key a merry tune,
While paper hats make us swoon.

Unveiling the Season

Pine needles fall like gentle rain,
As grandma yells, "Don't touch the grain!"
The ornaments are on display,
Except for one that rolled away.

The joyous shouts erupt like cheer,
While Elf shoes squeak right in your ear.
A game of charades with silly moves,
Got auntie laughing, oh how she grooves.

Echoes of Celebration

The fumblebumble of holiday cheer,
Half-baked cookies I hold dear.
A frosty window may reveal,
The neighbor's dog has learned to squeal.

With mittens stuck and hats askew,
Each moment shared feels fresh and new.
A chorus of giggles fills the air,
As we toast to mischief everywhere.

Flurries of Tradition

Snowflakes tumble, what a sight,
Laughter echoes through the night.
Uncle Joe's in his reindeer suit,
Chasing kids with a rubber boot.

Old carols muffled by the cheer,
Grandma's cookies disappear each year.
The cat's in the tree, oh what a feat,
With tinsel tangled around his feet.

Frosty falls, then tries to stand,
But slips right into a snowball band.
While siblings compete in a pie eating race,
With whipped cream flying all over the place!

As night falls, the lights twinkle bright,
A family circus, what a delight.
Laughing together, we break the norm,
In flurries of joy, our hearts stay warm.

Boundless Joy in the Twilight

Twinkling lights on every block,
Grandpa's snoring, oh what a shock!
Screaming kids wrapped in their toys,
Build snowmen shaped like all the boys.

The feast is set, but wait, oh dear,
Who let the dog taste the reindeer beer?
A toast to uncles with hair like fluff,
Who dance so weird, it's just enough!

With chestnuts roasting, a humorous twist,
Mom burns them all, yet we can't resist.
The tree leans low, it could almost fall,
As we mumble round to deck the hall!

In twilight's glow, our voices blend,
With joy that stretches, around each bend.
We laugh and cheer, as the night rolls on,
In this wacky wonderland, we're never done!

Radiance in the Silence

In the glow, we light the scene,
Winking bulbs, a festive sheen.
Pungent pies and cookies round,
Laughter echoes, joy is found.

Uncle Joe's got dance moves wild,
Cousins giggle, one's a child.
Tinsel tangled in her hair,
Who needs grace? We do not care!

The dog snatches all the treats,
While Grandma bakes with two left feet.
Snowflakes sprinkle, a frosty dance,
As we prance in our silly pants.

With jolly tunes, we all unite,
Singing off-key, but it feels right.
Friends and fam, we deck the place,
Bringing warmth, and lots of grace.

Twilight Gatherings

The clock strikes eight, the fun begins,
A never-ending chat as everyone spins.
Grandpa's stories take top prize,
Each tale more funny than the last surprise.

Frosty air and scarves galore,
Laughter spills through every door.
A snowball fight? Oh, what a sight!
As mittens fly, we laugh with delight.

A rogue puppy steals a shoe,
Our focus shifts, he seems brand new.
Hot drinks spill, and cheeks grow red,
The evening a whirlwind, we're far from dread.

With silly hats and light-hearted cheers,
We celebrate together, through giggles and tears.
A joyful night, with friends so dear,
Under twinkling lights, we spread the cheer.

Sweet Tidings in the Air

In a frenzy, the stockings hang,
What's inside? A jingle sang.
With silly games and antics bright,
We all embrace the starry night.

The fruitcake sits, a fabled foe,
Some take a bite, then swiftly go.
Caught in laughter, we take a stance,
At the oddest dish that steals the chance.

The cat climbs high, the tree's delight,
She knocks down baubles, oh what a sight!
Under the mistletoe, a cheeky wink,
An awkward kiss, we laugh and think.

As we gather round for one last toast,
To family and friends, we love the most.
With goodies shared and dreams to share,
We fill the air with joy so rare.

Hearthstone Revelry

Round the fire, we roast the treats,
S'mores fly high, no losses or defeats.
A marshmallow fight breaks out in glee,
Stickiness and giggles, oh what a spree!

The saga of socks, mismatched and bold,
A trendsetter? No, but brave and cold.
We dance to tunes that don't always rhyme,
Creating our rhythm, it's jolly time!

The lights flicker, a shadow dance,
We twirl and spin, all in a trance.
The joy of the night, it fills the room,
As we banish the darkness and let laughter bloom.

So here's to laughter, whimsy, and cheer,
With loved ones near, we hold them dear.
Through thick and thin, this night we keep,
A memory cherished, our hearts will leap.

Boughs of Green and Gold

In a cozy room, lights brightly twinkle,
The tree's not straight, it likes to crinkle.
Ornaments hang in a wobbly line,
Let's hope they stay, or they'll make us whine.

Bows are tied with a somehow thick flair,
One's stuck in the cat's fur, oh what a scare!
Tinsel's a frizz that's caught in a mess,
Our holiday cheer? It's a funny dress!

Sweet Aromas of Celebration

Snickerdoodles sizzling in the oven's embrace,
One's flying out, oh my! What a race!
Gingerbread men run with icing for shoes,
In the chaos of frosting, who'll win? Place your views.

Fruitcake's a mystery, a dense little block,
It's the only thing left, it refuses to talk.
The dog sniffs around, but stays far away,
Guess he knows something we all might betray!

Reflections in the Glass

With each sip of cheer, my uncle does hop,
He claims he can dance, though he might just flop.
The mirror reflects a jolly old chap,
Who's lost the remote; just give him a tap.

The children are giggling, they've built quite a mess,
Santa's lost in laughter, but who could guess?
Pudding's on the table, but wait, where's the cake?
Even the laughter's got frosting to bake!

Light and Laughter All Around

The twinkling lights seem to wiggle and sway,
Uncle Joe's jokes get funnier each day.
He's stuck in the tree, oh what a delight,
His head pops out, giving us quite a fright!

Laughter erupts like a bundle of socks,
An argument rises over holiday clocks.
But as we all gather, with hearts full of cheer,
It seems even the figgy has joined in the cheer!

Splendor of the Silent Night

In the glow of twinkling bulbs,
The kittens plot their great heist,
For the shiny baubles they love so much,
They think they're food, oh what a surprise!

The tree stands tall but shifty,
With ornaments that never stay put,
Every time we're not looking,
Down they go with a clumsy thud!

The cookies left for Santa's snack,
Nibbled by the raccoon next door,
The kids wake up to a feast of crumbs,
Santa's sleigh? Who needs that chore?

In the hush of winter's snowy cloak,
The laughter echoes, sharp and bright,
For amidst the flurry of mishaps proud,
Joy comes spilling out, pure delight!

Embracing the Chill

Bundled up like marshmallows,
We trek out to catch some snowflakes,
But halfway there, a snowball flies,
Right in my face - oh, for goodness' sake!

A snowman with a carrot nose,
Looks a lot like Uncle Fred,
With a broomstick slung on his shoulder,
Wiggles his arms - I think he's dead!

Frosty air and frosty talks,
As we sip cocoa with foam galore,
But someone bumped the mittens heap,
And now our fingers are a war!

Under strands of knitted scarves,
We stand with noses all aglow,
For in the chill, the warmth we find,
Is laughter shared in the frosty show!

Envelopes of Light

With paper, ribbons, and quirky tags,
Gifts piled high in secret delight,
The dog smells trouble, and oh to think,
We forgot to hide them out of sight!

Unwrapping presents like champions,
Tissues flying like confetti made,
But all I got was a pair of socks,
When did this jolly swap parade?

Grandma's cookies hit the table,
I sneak one, then another, oh dear,
But when I reach for one more, alas!
They're all just crumbs, what a terrible fear!

By the glow of the strings above,
We giggle with mouths full of cheer,
In the end, it's not what we received,
But the blunders that every year endear!

Memories Wrapped in Warmth

Gathered round with stories to tell,
Auntie sings like a cat on a spree,
Her notes hit high but bounces down low,
Bravo! Oh wait, now where's the key?

Brother's jokes are worse than ever,
His punchlines land with an awkward thud,
Yet we laugh until our sides ache,
As he mimes a snowman slipping in mud!

The fireplace crackles with humor,
As stockings fill with silly treats,
We pull out those ridiculous gifts,
And wear paper hats like fancy elites!

In a whirlwind of giggles and warmth,
These moments are treasure in time's own quilt,
So we raise our mugs of cheer here now,
For the joy and love that we have built!

The Sparkle of Hope in the Dark

In a room filled with twinkle and cheer,
Someone asked, "Is that my drink or a tear?"
The lights all shimmer, the food's on display,
But who stole the ham? Let's investigate today!

Laughter erupts as the dog steals a roll,
And uncle Lou's dancing, he's losing control.
We toss paper hats, and then aim for the tree,
This festive night, wild as wild can be!

The snow outside falls, a blanket of white,
We compete for the best, then we lose all our sight.
With eyes all a-widened, the snacks disappear,
And the jokes grow sillier, every minute, I cheer!

So here's to the secrets that make spirits soar,
To the mischief and magic, who could ask for more?
A sparkle of hope in the jolly old dark,
As we sing out the tune—oh, dear, where's my car key's
spark?

Silent Wishes Beneath the Stars

Under the twinkle of stars, how divine,
We whispered our wishes, with glasses of wine.
But wait! Is that Grandma, with mistletoe on?
Precision, my friends, she'll match you with Don!

The cookies are baking, and so is our pride,
But who let the cat in, oh what a wild ride!
He's dug through the ribbons, upturned the chair,
We thought we were wise, turns out, we're not quite fair!

The music is playing, a downright cute scene,
While siblings debate if the tree's really green.
We giggle and hug, throughout all the mess,
This night of sweet chaos is truly the best!

With laughter that echoes beneath heaven's light,
We count all our blessings and snooze all the night.
For silently wishing, with friends near and far,
Each chuckle, each smile, is a wish that's a star!

Flickering Shadows of Joy

In the corner, a glimmer, a hint of delight,
Dad's lost in the lights—can he even see right?
He's tangled in tinsel, what a sight to behold!
While the fruitcake's glaring, just too dense and too bold!

The kids are in triumph, they're scheming away,
On how to convince us that broccoli's gay.
Meanwhile, Aunt May's singing a song from the past,
If only the melody could carry her fast!

Shadows dance cheerfully, what chaos we start,
As Mom's yelling "Stop!" while the dog claims her heart.
A slip and a tumble, oh what a grand fall,
We're laughing and prancing, we'll have a ball!

So raise up your snacks, with a grin ear to ear,
Tonight is for laughter, for love, and good cheer.
Flickering joy in the warm, twinkling glow,
With such crazy stories, together we grow!

Harmonies of the Yuletide

A chorus of giggles fills up the whole room,
As the cousins debate on the size of the broom.
This broom's for good luck, or so they all say,
But no one will ask when it's cleaning out hay!

The table is laden with dishes galore,
But who's got the wine? It's gone—down the floor!
And Uncle's old sweater, oh how it does clash,
We're all in agreement, it's made of pure trash!

The tunes all are floating, but slightly off-key,
As features enraged sing with glee, "That's not me!"
A harmony joyful, with rhythm so bright,
That invites all the neighbors to join in tonight!

So here's to the laughter, the snickers and cheers,
The memories crafted throughout all the years.
With harmonies free, let the moments ignite,
We'll dance like we're silly till the morning's first light!

Lullabies of Tradition

In the corner, the lights do dance,
Mysteriously swaying, they take a chance.
Grandma's cookies are slightly burned,
Yet we laugh, for they are well-earned.

The jingle bells sound a bit off key,
A cat plays a solo, just let it be.
The socks on the mantle are mismatched flair,
Who needs matching? It's simply rare!

The gift tags wobble, none are quite right,
'To My Favorite Cousin' from a dog in sight.
The cocoa's like glue, but what's the fuss?
We sip and smile without much fuss.

As the clock strikes, we sing a tune,
While the dog fakes a yawn, under the moon.
So much joy, and a dash of glee,
Now let's pray there's no pasta for tea!

Firelit Reflections

The flames crackle softly, a pop and a hiss,
While Uncle Joe claims he's got a gift to miss.
A sweater so ugly, it makes us all cry,
Yet he grins like a kid, oh my, oh my!

Stories unfold that grow taller with age,
Of the snowball fight won by the fridge as a stage.
We laugh till we ache, it's quite the parade,
Who knew turkeys could still be delayed?

Outside the snow crafts a shiny façade,
While inside we're plotting a wild charade.
A pop quiz on songs, who knows all the notes?
And the ones who can't? They just ditch the coats!

With mugs raised high, we make silly toasts,
To the eggnog that's fizzy, then oops—it's the ghosts!
We join in the laughter, and hearts interlace,
In a world full of whacky, it's the jolly place!

Heartstrings in Harmony

A chorus of giggles at the tree's great tale,
Was it Mom or the cat that knocked down the mail?
With tinsel askew and ornaments bent,
We cherish these moments, so well-spent.

The mischief is found in each gift wrapped tight,
Who would give grandma a whack-a-mole fight?
The wrapping paper flies like confetti aglow,
Hidden snug 'neath the mess, the cat finds his show!

We sing festive tunes, off-key, we declare,
To the tunes of the night, we breathe in the air.
Our voices, a ruckus, a sweet lilting gale,
As we cheer for the stories and hope they won't fail.

In the warmth of the laughter, we find our own beat,
While the pizza's still cold, it can't be discreet.
So we raise all our forks for the joy we create,
With a dash of the goofy, we really can't wait!

Togetherness in the Glow

The lights look like fireflies having their ball,
While we get lost in the joy, the cheer, and the sprawl.
Some play air guitar on imaginary strings,
As our hearts share a laugh at the joy that it brings.

The dogs in their sweaters parade with such grace,
While the kids have their own secret, giggly place.
With marshmallows falling from cups filled with cheer,
The chaos just makes everything seem more dear!

The magic of family, a dance and a twirl,
Whispers of secrets shared with a swirl.
Each moment a treasure, a laugh or a jest,
In the glow of the night, we embrace it all best!

So here's to the wonders, the chaos and charm,
To laughter, shenanigans, and all that warms.
We'll wrap up this night in hugs that just flow,
Together we shine, like the lights that we know!

Songs Beneath the Silent Sky

The lights are twinkling, quite a show,
While grandma's twirling, moving slow.
The cat's in the tree, don't ask me how,
Just hope she won't knock it all down now.

The cookies are burning, oh what a smell,
Uncle Joe's loud, broke out his yell.
The music is cheesy, stuck in our heads,
At least we're not all still in our beds!

The gifts are all wrapped in paper galore,
At least the dog stopped chewing the door.
The laughter is bright, it fills up the room,
As we spy on the neighbors, on their broom.

With socks on our heads, we dance through the night,
The twinkle lights wobble, oh what a sight!
While cookies and sweets, they vanish away,
We'll laugh 'til we cry, come what may!

Embracing the Glimmer of Peace

Beneath the stars, we gather around,
Hiding the giggles, that burst out sound.
Hot cocoa spills, on the floor like a spree,
Did I just see a flying candy?

The dog in a sweater, thinks he's the king,
As we try to strum a makeshift-bling thing.
The kids sing off-key, yet cheerfully loud,
While I ponder if I should retire to the crowd.

The tales grow taller, as old folks declare,
About that one time they caught a big bear.
With each silly story, another drink cheers,
Even Santa may cringe at our wild years!

Laughter abounds, and joy fills the day,
With each silly mishap, we just want to play.
In this hilarious chaos, we find our sweet glee,
Together we smile, our hearts dancing free!

Radiant Tones of Love Unfolding

Demented reindeer, on their festive flight,
Down through the chimney, they scare with delight.
We're all in our PJs, with socks mismatched,
Jumping in joy—who needs a witchcraft?

A turkey that's dancing, or is it just me?
While Auntie attempts new recipes, oh jeez!
The fruitcake arrives, it bears quite the weight,
But grandad insists that it's worthy of fate.

We'll sing with abandon, although off the beat,
The neighbors are laughing; they think we're a treat.
Each silly mistake, turns into pure gold,
With warmth in our hearts, together we fold.

In this quirky gathering, we steer through the night,
Embracing the silliness, everything's right.
With joy in our voices, and smiles all around,
We cherish these moments, where laughter is found!

Twilight's Promise and Warmth

As twilight descends, the chaos begins,
With all of our cousins—what wild little sins!
The pets wear their hats, and the fridge goes boom,
While the oven is beeping, oh man, what a gloom!

We shiver with giggles, our cheeks growing red,
When Uncle Bob claims to have painted the shed.
With puns that could make any Grinch start to cheer,
We toast to the stories, and sip on our beer.

The snacks are a mess; sprinkles fly up,
While the children all fight over one big cup.
The tree starts to tilt like a dance on the floor,
But we wouldn't trade it for anything more!

Under the glow, our hearts feel so bright,
With dreams colored chipper, and laughter takes flight.
As the night spills the secrets, sweet memories arise,
In this jolly chaos, we find our surprise!

Illuminated Night with Laughter's Dance

In the glow, we strut and sway,
Socks mismatched, all in disarray,
Grandma's cookies make a mess,
But who cares? We're feeling blessed!

The tree's wonky, lights fall down,
Dad's wearing mom's old gown,
Uncle Joe sings off-key loud,
While we laugh, he feels so proud!

Hot cocoa spills on Auntie Sue,
Furry friends join in the crew,
Every sip, a splash of joy,
Holiday cheer, our favorite toy!

Outside snowflakes play a game,
But on this night, we're all insane,
With laughter ringing through the air,
This joyful chaos—beyond compare!

A Mosaic of Warmth and Wonder

Fluffy slippers dance on toes,
Mismatched hats, only goodness flows,
Pizza night with toppings flare,
Who knew cheese could fly through air?

Bouncing balls and singing loud,
As we celebrate, we're all proud,
Pasta noodles, lost in the fun,
A spaghetti battle has begun!

Chasing pets who steal the pie,
"Hey, that's mine!" we feign a cry,
But with giggles, joy does sprout,
In this night, there's no doubt!

With bright lights twinkling at night,
Our silly games are pure delight,
In every corner, laughter leans,
Mosaic made of giggling scenes!

Enchanted Glow of Hidden Wishes

Whispers of dreams in the airy space,
As silly elves join our embrace,
Karaoke night, we sing away,
With mics made of candy, hooray!

Dancing shadows twirl on walls,
Our wild shouts are the upbeat calls,
Laughter boxes under the bed,
Surprises waiting, brightly spread!

Chasing presents, wrapping spree,
Uncle Fred gets lost in glee,
Furry critters race on by,
In this charm, we all can fly!

Hidden wishes in a wink,
Magic swirls in every drink,
Tonight's the night we let it show,
A glow of joy, come join the flow!

Twinkling Spirits in the Chill

Frosty air and giggles high,
Snowballs thrown as we all try,
Laughter echoes through the trees,
Slipping, sliding, "Oh, look, freeze!"

Brightly dressed, a sight to see,
Funky sweaters, oh what glee,
Cookie dough fights, the best of all,
Sprinkles drop and cupcakes fall!

Furry friends in fluffy wraps,
Chasing tails and playful slaps,
Every mishap makes us grin,
In this riff, we all win!

With spirits twinkling in the night,
We forget the cold; it feels just right,
Join the cheer, embrace the thrill,
Laughter rings—let's dance until!

Radiant Embrace of Timeless Grace

In a corner, shadows prance,
While critters join the dance.
Laughter spills from every nook,
As pets eye the feast and look.

Hats and scarves, all jazzed up,
Sipping cocoa from a cup.
Uncle Fred sings the wrong tune,
Right under the bright balloon.

The tree leans a little too near,
A curious cat, oh dear!
With tinsel now on the floor,
How 'bout we sweep up some more?

Bring the jokes, let them fly,
As auntie flings pie up high.
Gifts are opened, chaos reigns,
We'll laugh until our sides complain.

Melodies Wrapped in Softness

With sleigh bells ringing wrong,
A choir sings a silly song.
The neighbor's dog, he howls along,
He thinks he's joined the throng.

In oversized sweaters, we twirl,
Tripping over garlands, oh swirl!
Hot cocoa spills, but who keeps score?
It's all fun, who could ask for more?

A prankster sneaks in some fruitcake,
But nobody's really awake.
We're all lost in a spicy haze,
What day is it? Who can appraise?

Once the laughter fills the air,
We share stories, none a care.
With love and quirks, we'll carry on,
Until we greet the break of dawn.

Dusk's Embrace and Gentle Light

The snowflakes swirled like a dance,
Did dad give that tree a chance?
It's sideways, leaning with pride,
A true fashion statement worldwide.

Grandma's recipe, oh so bold,
Fruits and nuts, a sight to behold.
With every nibble, we huff and sigh,
"How did this one ever fly?"

The clock strikes, it's time to cheer,
Grandpa snuck a secret beer!
He's humming tunes off-beat and loud,
Leading the most confused crowd.

With warming hugs and silly mess,
We toast each smile, we wish no less.
In bursts of giggles, we revel,
Under playful starry level.

Heartstrings Woven in Soft Glow

Gather 'round the flickering sights,
As wild tales take off in flights.
A fight breaks out for the last snack,
"Hey, I saw it first!" Yells back.

An elf costume makes Uncle shy,
While kids plead, "Just one more pie!"
A snowman stands, but not for long,
As a snowball flies, a little wrong.

Twirling in sweaters, clashing hues,
We own this party, no time for blues.
Pranks and giggles, mischief galore,
With joy that opens every door.

As the moon casts a cheeky glow,
We hope that you've enjoyed the show.
With hearts so full, we end the night,
Till next year's frolic and delight!

A Festival of Light and Harmony

Twinkling beams upon the tree,
Who knew they'd fight so eagerly?
Ornaments in a merry scam,
Cousin Joe just got the jam!

Laughter fills the clumsy air,
Grandma's dance, oh do beware!
Spinning treats right off the floor,
Watch out for that open door!

Festive hats all a bit askew,
Lost a friend, oh, where is Sue?
Silly twirls and fruity pies,
Why is Dad in Grandma's disguise?

Underneath the starlit night,
Mittens missing, what a sight!
Frolicking in the snow so bright,
Oops, that's Mom, not a snowman bite!

Starry Eyes and Warm Hearts

Sparkling treats and frosty cheer,
Who threw the cake, oh dear, oh dear!
Jingle bells with a squishy crunch,
Uncle Bob ate all the lunch!

Giggles bounce all 'round the room,
Did someone let the squirrel loom?
Laughter echoes in our midst,
Whispers of the Christmas twist!

Ribbons tangled, oh so bright,
What's that cat doing tonight?
Found a gift, oh what a stink,
Why's Grandpa wearing pink, I think?

Fizzy drinks and odd cheer mates,
Talking socks and looking late,
In the glow of festive charms,
Nobody minds the guard dog's barks!

The Gentle Glow of Kindness

Glow sticks mixed with fairy lights,
Who brought treats that look like frights?
Cheeseball towers, what a sight,
Who knew green could be so bright?

Naughty elves in mitten cheer,
Did you hear that laugh from near?
Whiskers twitch and tails wag fast,
Oh no, that's the family cat!

Mismatched socks upon the floor,
Here comes someone through the door!
Ray of warmth in funny ways,
Watch out for those turkey trays!

Silly songs 'til late at night,
Good intentions, what a fright!
In the joy of heartfelt times,
When did we start those silly rhymes?

Starlit Whispers of the Season

Underneath the twinkling skies,
Silly folks with shifty eyes,
A pie was thrown, oh what a sight,
Merry mishaps last all night!

Laughter drowns the frozen air,
Did Aunt Sue just start to share?
Lost the cue for songs in spree,
Cousins jamming off-key glee!

Reindeer snacks all found the ground,
Watch it, that's my favorite sound!
Chasing lights and running feet,
Who spiked Dad's eggnog treat?

Playful whispers in the dark,
Who brought home the dancing spark?
In the spirit, laugh and play,
Funny tales that won't decay!

Whispered Dreams by Firelight

On winter nights, we gather round,
With whispers floating, laughter bound.
A cat jumps high, a dog will chase,
As marshmallows melt in cozy space.

The socks we hung, all mismatched glee,
A magical scene for all to see.
With chocolate stains on every face,
Who needs perfection in this place?

A tale of Santa, just for cheer,
Yet Uncle Bob still drinks his beer.
We giggle loud and sing off-key,
A jolly mess, just let it be.

In glow of light, the spirit's clear,
Even grumpy Auntie cracks a cheer.
With hearts so full, we'll dance tonight,
Embracing joy by firelight.

Illumination of the Heart

The glow from snacks lights up the room,
Ignored the veggies, they stay in gloom.
The punch is spiked, oh what a thrill,
A toast to chaos, let's get our fill.

Grandma's jokes, they never fail,
Like how she tripped on her own tail.
With laughter ringing through the day,
It's all quite normal in our way.

We'll wear our sweaters, oh so bright,
Look like a gaggle in plain sight.
Though colors clash, it's quite the art,
A silly fashion warms the heart.

With mischief brewing in the air,
A snowball fight, do we dare?
No peaceful night is in the chart,
Just silly fun and joy to start.

Tinsel and Twilight

The roof's adorned with odds and ends,
Like something made by awkward friends.
The lights flash madly, quite a scene,
With colors bright, like candy's sheen.

A squirrel's feast, oh what a sight,
As he claims our snack in broad daylight.
While we are stuck in giggles' grip,
He's living life, a heist on his trip.

We dance like fools, crank up the cheer,
Our neighbor's dog joins in, oh dear!
With tunes so jumbled, round we go,
The spirit wild, in high and low.

As midnight strikes, we'll clink our cups,
And toast to all the silly ups.
With stories shared and hearts so free,
Nonsense reigns in jubilee.

Harmonies in the Frost

The snowflakes dance beneath the light,
As penguin socks bring pure delight.
A hot tub party in the snow,
We splash and giggle, 'frosty flow.'

With silly hats and boots so neat,
A snowman's made of cold retreat.
His smile's gone, the dog took haste,
Now look, it's soup, a snowy waste!

A chorus forms, our voices clash,
Out of tune, oh what a smash!
Yet sing we must, with steely grit,
A night so wild, we'll never quit.

As laughter echoes through the night,
With frosty breath and pure delight.
We'll raise a glass to joy and fun,
The night is young, let's not yet run.

Festooned with Cheer

Twinkling lights dance in the air,
Pine trees wear hats, oh what a flare!
Grandma's cookies—a gooey delight,
Makes everyone jolly, by day and by night.

Socks on the mantle, what a bold claim,
Can they fit? Who knows! It's a silly game.
A jingle bell choir sings off-key tunes,
But laughter and giggles fill all the rooms.

Elves on the shelves have secrets to spill,
They plot mischief while munching on quill.
A reindeer with glitter, oh what a sight,
Forgetting his manners in joyous delight.

In this season of chaos, we raise our cheer,
With mishaps and laughter, year after year.

Illuminated Traces of Delight

The snowman wobbles, his carrot a mess,
With a hat too big and a smile, no less.
Children in pajamas, sleepy but bold,
Hoping for magic more precious than gold.

Muffins are burning, oh what a smell!
Dad thinks he's a chef; we can never tell.
Whispers of secrets from under the bed,
Chasing the cat as it flees with dread.

Singing of joy, with hiccups and snorts,
The family gathers, in mismatched shorts.
A tree full of trinkets, some hang on for dear,
While others fall down, never meant to appear.

In this grand celebration, humor's the key,
With laughter and smiles, we all dance with glee.

Unwrapped Joy

Boxes and ribbons, a total wreck,
Whispers of chaos, what did we expect?
Scissors and tape, wrapped tight with a bow,
But Uncle Joe's watch? It was a big no-show.

Paper confetti flies high in the air,
Some under the couch, most everywhere.
Grandpa's old sweater, a sight to behold,
Perfectly fitted for a mannequin, bold.

Presents are opened with shouts of delight,
Then wrapped up again like a Christmas kite.
Giggles burst forth like popcorn in pan,
A sticky mess left by the excited clan.

What matters is laughter, togetherness tight,
In this bundle of joy, so merry, so bright.

Voices in the Stillness

Snowflakes fall gently, like whispers of cheer,
Echoes of laughter fill up the year.
With cookies forgotten, and milk left behind,
Dreams of tomorrow, in our hearts entwined.

The dog steals the turkey, oh what a sight,
While Auntie's knitting grows tangled with fright.
Gather 'round, everyone, let's share a few tales,
Of how the cat knocked over the festive gales.

In the still of the night, when the world seems to pause,
Our hearts beat together, just because.
With voices of merriment, we fill up the space,
Grateful for moments that time can't erase.

So here's to the chaos, the love and the cheer,
The stories we cherish, each glorious year.

Glow in the Frost

Little lights twinkle, dance all around,
Frosty breath giggles, what fun to be found!
Snowflakes are stubborn, they cling to your nose,
Chasing them down, oh how everyone glows!

Hot cocoa's steaming, marshmallows afloat,
Joyfully laughing, we wiggle and gloat.
With frosty fingers, we wave to the moon,
Who knows what mischief tomorrow will swoon?

Socks on our pets, they're strutting with pride,
Combining with chaos, oh what a wild ride!
The snowman stands guard, in a hat that won't stick,
He'll challenge the sunlight, we'll see who is quick!

Whipped cream disasters, squirted too high,
Mom's trying to catch it, oh my, oh my!
In the winter wonderland, laughter meets cheer,
So let's dance 'round the lights, with nothing to fear!

Whispered Melodies of Night

In a cozy corner, we gather so tight,
Singing odd jingle tunes that burst with delight.
Grandma's got rhythm, but should stick to her chair,
With cat on her lap, it's a quirky affair!

The tree's a bit lopsided, top heavy and bright,
Ornaments wobble, oh what a sight!
Dogs are all tangled in garlands of gold,
Cats watch with mischief, their plans to unfold.

Hot pie on the table, too hot to bite down,
A race to the oven, my goodness, it's brown!
Eggnog explodes, well it's not quite a pour,
We're slipping in laughter, and oh how we roar!

Outside the wind whistles a curious tune,
While we snicker and giggle under the moon.
Mischief and magic, oh what can we make?
These whispered nights, full of sweetness and shake!

Light's Embrace on Winter's Hearth

Gather 'round, buddies, it's time for a game,
Mismatched socks be turned into a claim!
With laughter and stories that stretch time anew,
Tickling our ribs, as we share all we view.

The dog's snoring loudly, a reindeer so bright,
His dreams contain wonders of cookies tonight.
Chasing the shadows, we jump and we prance,
As the marshmallow craze leads us all to dance!

Tinsel's a treasure, but what a disaster,
The cat's on the prowl, and he's climbing faster.
With each little sparkle, we echo our cheer,
This festive calamity brings us all near!

Hot snacks and giggles, oh what a great mess,
The party's contagious, a holiday bless.
So let's take a moment, embrace all the fun,
These friends and these laughs are what makes us as one!

Tinsel Dreams and Midnight Gleams

In the kitchen chaos, we bake and we cheer,
Flour's in our hair, but we're full of good cheer!
With cookies a'burning, we need a quick fix,
Chefs in our aprons, it's a crafty mix!

Jingle bell socks dance on our merry feet,
Knocking over cocoa, a chocolatey treat!
The fridge has become a hiding place now,
For the s'mores that are secret, oh boy, take a bow!

Outside there's laughter, it's echoing bright,
As snowballs fly swift in this wonderful night.
Snowmen are wobbling, they're losing their form,
But joy in this moment keeps our hearts warm!

Under the starlight, the fun never lags,
Merriness jangles in our cozy rags.
Tinsel dreams flutter, oh what a sweet fate,
With giggles and winks as we close the estate!

Echoes of Winter's Embrace

Snowflakes dance in the air,
Laughter bubbles everywhere.
Frosty breath on a cheek,
Tickles make us squeak.

Mittens lost in the fray,
Chasing snowmen all day.
Hot cocoa in a cup,
Silly marshmallows jump up.

Jingle bells on my toes,
But my nose is red like a rose.
As we shimmy and sway,
Winter games are here to play.

Giggles echo through the night,
Hope your snowball's not too tight!
With every twinkling light,
We warm up for our delight.

Luminary Wishes

The stars are winking bright,
Come join the silly fight!
Some say 'more is best',
But wait, there's pumpkin zest!

Pine scents fill the air,
While squirrels dance without a care.
Not a creature is stirring,
Except for my cat's purring!

Lights flicker, then they glow,
Watch as my uncle bends low.
Tripped over his very shoe,
"Oh dear, what's new?" he flew!

We roast marshmallows wide,
With friends all gathered side by side.
Laughter comes and emotions blend,
Holiday cheer won't ever end!

Harmony in the Hush

Quiet comes as the snow sinks,
Who knew we'd lose our jinx?
With a sled and little cheer,
We laugh like no one's near.

A whisper here, a giggle there,
Sometimes we even share a stare.
Snowmen with carrot noses,
Are really just funny poses!

Grandma calls from the door,
"Dinner's ready! Bring no more!"
We're still busy having fun,
But I guess we'll run and shun!

Through the frosty field we glide,
Each moment filled with joy and pride.
As the sun sets, we won't forget,
When winter nights are our best bet.

Frosted Gratitude

Presents piled under the tree,
Who knew it would bumble so free?
Wrapping paper flies like confetti,
With bows that fit all too petty!

Chase the cat, it's not a toy,
It's sure to bring us all some joy.
Grandpa tries to pull a prank,
Socks in each box, oh how we tank!

Cookies gone in a blink,
Not a crumb left, don't you think?
Milk mustache on my face,
As I laugh and try to race.

Cheers to all the quirky things,
Like gnomes with tights and silly rings.
In laughter, we find our groove,
Thankful hearts, we sure improve!

Luminescence of Togetherness

Flickering lights dance on the wall,
Grandma's wig just took a fall.
The turkey's on the floor, oh dear,
Uncle Joe is guzzling beer.

Gifts wrapped poorly make us grin,
Cats are climbing - where to begin?
The kids are bouncing off the walls,
While Dad attempts his festive calls.

Laughter echoes through the night,
Socks are mismatched, but that's alright.
Mom's burnt cookies taste like bait,
But who could ever hesitate?

An ornament that has gone rogue,
Still, we gather close - be it fog.
With every chuckle, warmth's bestowed,
In our hearts, the joy is sowed.

Frosted Echoes of Cheer

Snowflakes land on Grandpa's hat,
His stories always make us spat.
A reindeer wearing neon shades,
As wild mishaps our night parades.

Silly sweaters bring a smile,
While dance moves spark a festive style.
The eggnog's strong, we take a sip,
And watch Aunt Sue take a trip.

Jingle bells that sound off-key,
Yet no one's really let it be.
We launch snowballs, aiming low,
And bickering over who will throw.

Late-night snacks are piled high,
With crumbs that raise our hopes to fly.
Though mushy memories take their place,
We wrap the night with cheerful grace.

Nightfall Serenade of the Heart

Under twinkling stars we sing,
To a tune that makes our hearts swing.
Deck the halls with blunders bold,
As stories of our past unfold.

A pet parrot starts to squawk,
Interrupting our festive talk.
While gifts grow legs and run away,
We laugh until the break of day.

Fuzzy socks become a race,
Each new pair brings on a craze.
As we tumble, giggling loud,
We overflow with joy, so proud.

Warm embraces steal the show,
Our silly faces all aglow.
In this chaos, we find our cheer,
Keeping each other close and near.

Hearthside Reveries and Soft Light

By the fire, we roast some treats,
As marshmallows scatter like small feats.
A ghost of laughter fills the air,
While Cousin Billy pulls a chair.

Grandpa snores and shakes the floor,
Oh no, not the Christmas decor!
Twinkling lights are dimmed with glee,
As we compete for best hot tea.

The night is young, the jokes flow free,
With every wink, a new decree.
The neighbor's cat leaps up in fright,
As we plan our holiday flight.

Mom's secret recipe's a flop,
The kids just giggle and won't stop.
Yet in this merry, crazy fight,
We find our glow in hearts so bright.

Soft Light

A Santa hat that's way too big,
On Grandpa's head, it does a jig.
With every clap and joyful cheer,
We toast to moments we hold dear.

A puppy wrapped in paper green,
He's wrestling gifts, a sight unseen.
Pine needles drop, a needle fight,
As we twirl around with pure delight.

The carols sung in silly tones,
Echo laughter, not just moans.
With mismatched socks and candy canes,
We dance through all our joyful gains.

Huddled close, we share our tales,
With silly jokes that tip the scales.
In every grin, and every spark,
We weave a warmth to beat the dark.

Cherished Radiance

In a room lit by twinkling sparks,
A cat eyes the tree and its glimmering marks.
With a swish of its tail, down the ornaments fly,
As we shout, 'Look out!' while we burst into cry.

Mistletoe hangs low with a wink and a grin,
A cousin approaches, ready to win.
But he trips on his feet, and oh what a sight,
Kissing the floor, not a girl, but delight!

Cookies baked hard as rocks, what a treat,
We laugh as we chew, daring to eat.
With milk that's been spiked—just a little—don't fret,
We'll dance around fridges, leave no room for regret.

So gather 'round closely, let the tales unfold,
Of moments so goofy, we just can't be told.
For in this bright bubble of warmth and of cheer,
We cherish the laughter that rings loud and clear.

Elysium of merriment

The jingle bells jangle, oh what a parade,
In socks that are mismatched and greatly displayed.
As Uncle Joe's snoring plays a sweet serenade,
We plot pranks and tricks that shall never degrade.

With holiday sweaters that itch like a bear,
We huddle together, all warmth, none to spare.
A cousin winks slyly, with something in hand,
This secret is juicy—it's not what we planned!

Gingerbread houses with icing galore,
But the dog has a taste for the roof we adore.
We shout and we giggle, while he scampers away,
Chasing him down feels like it's Christmas Day!

So raise up your glass filled with fizzy delight,
Toast to this madness, the sheer joy, the fight.
With each laugh a treasure, more gold than can gleam,
In a realm of mischief, we dance and we scheme!

Timeless Traditions

Each year we gather, a festive brigade,
With stories retold and inside jokes displayed.
One uncle goes fishing, but always with flair,
With tales of the one that just slipped through his care.

The fire crackles softly, but soon is drowned out,
By five kids who're shouting—and nothing but doubt.
In a flurry of pillows—a snowballing fight,
Who will claim victory? It's all pure delight!

Pudding that quivers like jelly on fire,
Is served up with laughter; it's all we desire.
With postcards from cousins who failed to show,
We plug in a webcam, turn the chaos to glow.

So hand me the gift that you've wrapped with such care,
Then watch while I struggle to open it, there.
For each funny moment—so quirky, so neat,
Is a page in our book that feels just like a treat.

Encircled by Happiness

With bright lights and laughter, we dance and we sway,
In a circle of friends who turned up for the play.
One slips and goes tumbling, who knew it would burn?
The cocoa erupts, as we all take our turn.

Eggnog connoisseurs, they boast of their skill,
With recipes scrawled on a napkin—what thrill!
But the secret is lounging in each of their cups,
It's too sweet to sip, yet we drink all the lumps!

As the clock nears the hour for wishes to fling,
We giggle, we snicker, at the joy that we bring.
With hugs and warm wishes, we laugh until dawn,
In a haze of good fun—what tale we are drawn!

So lift up your spirits, join the vibrant throng,
For cherishing jest is where we all belong.
In silliness woven, our hearts find their way,
In a glow of connection—the merriest play!

Evening Whisperings

Twinkling lights on frosty eaves,
Pine needles tickle, oh how we heave.
A cat on the tree, it's quite a sight,
As we giggle softly in the night.

Grandma's fruit cake, such a delight,
Tastes like a mystery, every bite.
Uncle Joe's socks, they surely glow,
With patterns that dance and steal the show.

The dog steals cookies, then blames the cat,
As grandpa snores with a laugh and a spat.
Oh, what a time, filled with glee,
As we toast marshmallows, just wait and see!

Joyful mischief fills every room,
As laughter and chaos begin to bloom.
So raise a glass, and cheer aloud,
For this wacky night, we're truly proud!

Emblems of Joyous Nights

Glittering globes swing and sway,
While crumpled wrapping papers play.
The jingle of bells from the fridge strikes,
As cold pizza steals the holidays' likes.

Mom's secret recipe is a hoot,
With cookies shaped like an ugly boot.
With sprinkles that somehow just flew,
It's a holiday wonder we've stumbled into.

The tree has more tinsel than ever,
As dad's on the floor with a grumpy endeavor.
With ornaments hung with a quirky flair,
And grandma's dance moves can give you a scare!

Toasting with cider that tastes like glue,
As we sing tunes that are off-key too.
Laughter and joy fill up the air,
In this merry madness, we all deeply care!

Celebratory Shimmers

Lights on the roof make squirrels lose track,
As they tumble and roll on the old snack pack.
With friends at the door, ready to cheer,
And in pjs that come from last year.

Mismatched socks and hats askew,
A game of charades leads to endless boo!
From three-legged races to cake that's a flop,
We'll giggle and laugh till we all drop.

Radio blares out a tune gone wrong,
While we join in with a chorus so strong.
A cat in a bow tie leads the dance,
As the night unfolds, it's pure happenstance.

Wrapping gifts with all of our might,
And finding them empty in morning light.
Exchanging our blunders with cheers and sighs,
This joyous season is the biggest surprise!

Chimes Through the Frost

The shimmer of night fills us with cheer,
As we dance 'round the fridge, no hint of a beer.
With a chorus of giggles bouncing around,
And grandma's wild tales seem heaven-bound.

Frosty fingers unlock silly secrets,
Turning the truth into curious beliefs.
Dad's festive sweater is a sight to behold,
With blinking lights, it's ridiculously bold!

The kids paint the snow with colors so bright,
While we sip hot cocoa, our lips in delight.
The puppy does flips in his tiny red hat,
And the mistletoe's lost in a funny spat.

So laughter dances along with the night,
As we cuddle and chat till the morning light.
With hearts full of joy and silly little bets,
Every moment we share, we'll never forget!

Light from the Abyss

In a room full of twinkling cheer,
A cat dives in the gifts, oh dear!
With ribbons tangled and boxes ajar,
She claims the glory, a feline star.

The snacks are piled high, too nice,
But watch out for that clever mice!
They're dancing 'round the cookies near,
Making our laughter much too clear.

Grandma's sweater is quite a sight,
With patterns bold, oh what a fright!
She prances 'round, all loud and bright,
Her holiday spirit a sheer delight.

So grab a plate, stay for a while,
Join in the fun, and share a smile!
For in this chaos, joy will thrive,
And the laughter keeps our spirits alive.

Joyful Voices in the Chill

Outside the snow is swirling down,
But inside the groove, we dance around!
With voices loud, and laughter near,
We serenade, slurring the cheer.

Hot cocoa spills, who made this mess?
Who knew joy could cause such stress?
We'll toast to harmony and silly fights,
While mugs collide like merry knights.

The tree's adorned with quirky flair,
A sock hanging from the highest hair.
We sing off-key but can't complain,
Our spirits soar like a runaway train.

So grab your friends, it's time to jest,
With joyful hearts, we are truly blessed.
We'll laugh and cheer throughout the night,
For in this silliness, all feels right.

Warmth Wrapped in Wonder

When the sky is dark and cheeks are red,
We gather around, the tales are spread.
With story twist and laughter bold,
It's not just tradition, but magic untold.

Pine-scent hangs, but so does the pie,
A slice for you, oh my, oh my!
With crumbs on shirts, and icing on chins,
We crown the night with joyful grins.

Grandpa's telling tales of yore,
While Auntie dances, always asking for more.
Mixing punch and mischief too,
It surely feels like a wild zoo!

We raise a cup, to cheer and play,
Let's make these memories, come what may.
For in this warmth, our hearts align,
With quirky fun, all things divine.

Stars Above the Hearth

Underneath the lights so bright,
We gather 'round, such a silly sight!
With goofy hats and tangled mistletoe,
Our holiday spirit is all aglow.

The jokes we tell, oh how they flow,
And oh, the dances—who could know?
With every twirl, a mishap's sparked,
Yet laughter lingers, joyfullyarked.

We hang our socks with reckless flair,
Will gifts be sugary? Will they be bare?
But the real treasure, once again,
Is each other's laughter, our true gain.

So let us toast, to joy and cheer,
With every giggle, we draw near.
For in this crazy, zany night,
Our hearts are full, the world feels right.

The Warmth of Shared Moments and Joy

In the corner, a pot roast spins,
While Uncle Fred dances, the chaos begins.
Kids giggle and chase on the floor,
Grandma's yelling, "You can't eat more!"

The dog steals a sock, and the cat takes a dive,
Amidst all the laughter, we feel so alive.
Hot cocoa spills, but we don't really care,
It's a win-win as we share the affair.

A game of charades brings out hidden skills,
And Auntie Sue's jokes give us all the chills.
Wrapped gifts tossed aside with delight,
As we share our stories, the joy feels just right.

With each little mishap, we chuckle and cheer,
Mom's secret recipe; we'll never get near.
In this merry chaos, our hearts sing out clear,
Together in humor, we hold one another dear.

A Light for Every Wish

In a sea of ribbons, the mischief begins,
As pets make a dash for the sweets and the pins.
Children write lists, their dreams stretching wide,
While Dad's in the corner, dressed up with pride.

Glimmers of laughter, they bounce off the walls,
A cacophony rings as the bell gently calls.
"Ho-ho-ho!" echoes, while the cat rolls her eyes,
Survival is key when there's fun in the skies.

Lights strung in circles, a twist here or there,
As Grandma concocts her odd festive flair.
Just don't let her near the fondue again,
The last time, we thought we'd never eat then!

Wishes fly high, can you see them take flight?
Mom's lost the scissors — it vanished in fright!
But laughter erupts as we gather to play,
'Cause the best kind of magic is found in our sway.

Glowing Nights

Under the twinkle of lights overhead,
A fountain of giggles where joy's never dead.
A cat in a hat? What a whimsical sight,
With yarn on her tail, she takes off in flight.

As we bake and we munch, a cookie bares a smile,
And chocolate chips vanish in the blink of a mile.
Dad can't quite follow the rhythms we share,
But we love his attempts; he's got style, we swear!

Mismatched socks wander across the wide floor,
A whirlwind of colors, who could ask for more?
We jingle our bells with clumsy delight,
Concerts of chaos, our hearts feel so light.

The mischief and laughter — a beautiful mess,
Finding joy in the moments, we all feel so blessed.
So here's to the glowing in each tiny spark,
In the laughter we echo, we're lighting the dark.

Melodies of December

As the winter winds howl, we huddle in twos,
A chorus of voices, with mismatched old shoes.
Grandpa strums something that's terribly flat,
But we all join in, and he doesn't know that.

With rubbery reindeer doing leaps on the rug,
And hot pies that suddenly prefer to hug.
The kids sing off-key, it's a jubilant sound,
While the cookies hide well, without making a sound.

Dancing around in our socks on the floor,
As puppy attempts to sneak out for a tour.
O'er spilling the drinks, we all laugh 'till we cringe,
To the joy of togetherness, we'll never infringe.

So let's raise a glass to this wacky mix,
In chaos and laughter, we find all our kicks.
For the season brings warmth, through giggles and cheer,
In these bustling moments, we hold all so dear.

Harmonies of Hearth and Home

Lights flicker with a wink,
The cat's plotting a heist.
Treats hide where you don't think,
In socks? That's quite the advice!

Grandma dances in her chair,
Spills cocoa on her feet.
The dog thinks it's a fair
To snag the marshmallow treat!

Oh, Uncle Joe's out of tune,
He sings louder with each sip.
Like a howler dog's full moon,
We all cringe then let it rip!

As laughter fills the room,
And socks all start to match,
We share the joyful gloom,
With every mishap, a scratch.

Night's Soft Embrace

Twinkling lights in the frosty air,
A squirrel gave the tree a scare.
Hiding snacks amidst the brights,
His heist went better in the nights.

Snowflakes fall, oh what a sight,
But Dad's stuck in a snowball fight.
While Mom's baking cookies round,
A sweet scent spreads, then falls to ground!

Siblings giggle, then they flee,
While puppy chases after me.
He trips and lands with a flop,
Now he's part of the snow, whoops, plop!

Head to toe in winter gear,
We make snowmen filled with cheer.
But somehow, one lost a hat,
Now it looks like a chubby cat!

Stories Beneath the Stars

Under the night, we gather tight,
With tales of gnomes in silly flight.
Grandpa claims he once saw one,
But he drank too much, oh what fun!

Midgets in red, like dashing sprites,
Bring gifts of socks and holiday lights.
A legend says they dance with glee,
But we just see them spill iced tea!

The moon's giggling, we join in,
With every tale, a raucous din.
"Just one more story!" we loudly plead,
Till silence falls—oh yes, indeed!

And as the night begins to fade,
Someone's snoozing—a grand charade.
We tiptoe past with quiet glares,
Not to wake them, don't you dare!

Luminous Journeys

Starry hats upon our heads,
While we trip over fluffy beds.
This bright light shines, oh dear,
A raccoon stole my sandwich here!

With every squeak, the laughter hums,
As we dance to ticklish drums.
If we fall, we land with flair,
And giggle, rolling without care!

Hot chocolate spills, drenching shoes,
How'd the mess come from our snooze?
But all mistakes are part of fun,
And holiday cheer has just begun!

Together we roam, hearts all aglow,
With sparkly hats and ten pairs, whoa!
As the sun peeks in for the morn,
A final dance, with joy we're born!

Songs of the Radiant

The lights are bright, they flicker and dance,
As socks hang tight, in a silly romance.
Elves in the kitchen, mix up a strange brew,
'Taste test' they shout, as it spills on the stew.

Gifts wrapped in paper, all shiny and bold,
With frills and with bows, more cute than of old.
A dog on the tree, what a sight to behold,
As laughter erupts, our stories retold.

Mittens on faces, a cat on the floor,
The snowflakes come down, but we're still needing more.

Hot cocoa spills over, marshmallows collide,
As we join in the fun, and the giggles are wide.

A jolly old fellow, quite round in his chair,
With cookies and milk, his belly in flair.
He jams to the tunes, sparkly and cute,
But trips on the rug, "I meant to, it's true!"

Festive Echoes Across the Land

The music is loud, with some jingles and chimes,
A turkey's gone rogue, causing all sorts of crimes.
Uncles in sweaters, as bright as a sun,
Dancing like penguins, oh what foolish fun!

A tree in the corner, a star way too tall,
With tinsel and baubles that beg you to fall.
Kids hiding presents where no one can peek,
Cheese sticks and giggles, the secrets we keep.

The snowman's not standing, he's melting away,
With a big smile asking if it's time to play.
Hot dogs in stockings, who would've a thought?
The joy and the laughter, together they fought!

As muffled laughter travels through the night,
We sing all our tunes, none perfect, but right.
The heart of the season, we share with a grin,
All chaos and joy, reflected within.

Memories of Frosted Mirth

A parade of odd folks, all gathered around,
While cookies and giggles that some have renowned.
The lights on the house flash colors so bright,
And Grandma, it seems, lost her wig in the fight.

With hats that are silly and shoes two sizes wide,
We stumble and bumble, like we're on a ride.
A pie that exploded, who saw it? Oh dear!
While laughter rings out, it's quite clear we're here.

Chasing the cat, who's just trying to hide,
As ribbons go flying, this family can't bide.
We toast with our mugs, filled to the brim,
In this juicy chaos, we're all feeling grim!

As bedtime approaches, we smile and we say,
"Tomorrow will bring us more trouble to sway!"
In warm, glowing hearts, memories ignite,
With frost in the air, we breathe in delight.

Whispers in the Gathering

The best time of year, it's loud and it's bright,
With stories and tales, each one quite a sight.
A chicken in charge of the barbecue cheer,
While the dog steals the food as he's sweating with fear.

Colorful parcels stacked high on a chair,
As Grandpa's dressed up, with flair to spare.
"Too much eggnog!" he says, then trips on a toy,
And we laugh at it all, oh what holiday joy!

We scatter our wishes like confetti on snow,
Through hot, chocolate circles, where wild spirits grow.
The snacks may be whipped cream, but we don't really
care,
For in chaos we find joy, and simple love to share.

As the night gets older, our stories unfold,
Bringing laughter and warmth, treasures more than gold.
So gather around, let's toast one more time,
To fun-loving moments, our lives in their prime!

Flickers of Hope

In a room filled with cheer, lighting goes astray,
A flicker and a shudder, then my pants catch a ray!
I jump and I dance, all while holding my drink,
With each clumsy twirl, I start to rethink.

The dog in the corner is having a blast,
He finds tinsel to chew, running wild and fast.
The cats are in hiding, both glaring and mewing,
While I pet my own head, confused and skewing.

The snacks are now melting, the punch has gone flat,
The cookies on the table resemble a mat.
I try to impress with a grand festive song,
Yet I trip over gifts and keep singing wrong!

But laughter erupts as we all share a joke,
While the lights start to dim and my uncle strokes smoke.
Next year I'll be smarter, or so I imply,
As we can't help but giggle 'til the evening says bye.

Yuletide Spirals

Round and round we go, with laughter in the air,
Tangled lights are flying, oh dear, what a affair!
With each twist and turn, I stumble, I fall,
The garland my guide, as I head for the wall.

The tree wobbles gently, as we try to adorn,
But I can't find the star, so we settle for corn.
Each bauble and ornament is stuck on my shoe,
I swear they're alive, what a hangout for two!

Underneath all the chaos, the dog wants a treat,
He snags my last cookie, oh how he's discreet.
With giggles and shrieks, we create quite the scene,
With joy all around, like a festive machine!

So here's to the spirals, the mess and the fun,
With laughter and chaos, the day's just begun.
As we toast to the madness, our spirits on high,
We'll grin through the mayhem, and let time fly by.

Serenade of the Season

The songs fill the air, but harmony's lost,
My aunt hits a note, like a cat got frost.
We smile and we giggle, through off-key delight,
As high notes go missing, we sing on despite!

The kids take the stage, in hats far too big,
They twirl and they sway like a small dancing pig.
With each silly movement, they bring up the pie,
And dad just can't stand it, almost wants to cry.

Around me the laughter, it rings loud and clear,
As someone trips over the joy (and the beer).
The folks gather close, raising glasses of cheer,
While one shouts a toast to the whiskers of deer!

So let music ring out, with squeaks and with giggles,
We'll embrace the mishaps, the laughter, the wiggles.
We'll serenade each other, no matter the tune,
'Til the stars start to twinkle and the night sings its boon!

Glistening Paths of Joy

Through the window I peek, and what do I see?
A raccoon in the yard, dancing under a tree.
With a sparkle of mischief, it winks back at me,
As it snags a wrapped present, oh what glee!

We bustle inside with our schmooze and our cheer,
While searching for warmth, and do I smell beer?
The roast is now singing, a charred lullaby,
We'll savor the flavors, we won't even cry!

The lights start to flicker, just like my last sock,
A visit from Uncle, in a mismatched frock.
He's jiving around, with dance moves so bold,
We all join in, as the stories unfold!

So here's to the laughter, the joy and the mess,
In a world full of quirks, we each feel so blessed.
With paths that are glistening, we stroll hand in hand,
Gathered in warmth, a merry, silly band!

Milton Keynes UK
Ingram Content Group UK Ltd.
UKHW020044271124
451585UK00012B/1042